ERIC THE RED

The Vikings Sail the Atlantic

ERIC THE RED

The Vikings Sail the Atlantic

Dr. Anne Millard

RSVP

RAINTREE
STECK-VAUGHN
PUBLISHERS
The Steck-Vaughn Company

Austin, Texas

Published by Raintree Steck-Vaughn Publishers, an imprint of Steck-Vaughn Company

Editors: Su Swallow, Shirley Shalit
Designer: Neil Sayer
Production: Jenny Mulvanny
Consultant: Charles Wetzel, Drew University

Maps and illustrations: Brian Watson, Linden Artists

Library of Congress Cataloging-in-Publication Data
Millard, Anne.
    Eric the Red: the Vikings sail the Atlantic / Anne Millard.
        p.   cm. — (Beyond the horizons)
    Includes bibliographical references.
    Summary: Describes the life of the Vikings, both at home and abroad, their boat-building and navigational skills, and their connection to England, Vinland, and Russia.
    ISBN 0-8114-7252-3
        1. Vikings — Juvenile literature. 2. Northmen — Juvenile literature. [1. Vikings.]
    I. Title. II. Series: Beyond the horizons.
DL65.M55   1994
940.1'4—dc20   93-26113
                                                                          CIP AC

Printed in Hong Kong
Bound in the United States
1 2 3 4 5 6 7 8 9 0 LB 99 98 97 96 95 94 93

Acknowledgments

For permission to reproduce copyright material the author and publishers gratefully acknowledge the following:

Cover (middle left, bottom right and far right) Ronald Sheridan, Ancient Art & Architecture Collection, (top left) Michael Holford, (bottom left) Werner Forman Archive/Statens Historiska Museum, Stockholm, (bottom middle) Werner Forman Archive/British Museum **Title page** e.t. archive **page 4** (top left and right) Ronald Sheridan, Ancient Art & Architecture Collection, (bottom left) Michael Holford **page 5** Ronald Sheridan, Ancient Art & Architecture Collection **page 6** (top) Mohamed Amin/Robert Harding Picture Library, (bottom) Ronald Sheridan, Ancient Art & Architecture Collection **page 7** (bottom) Robert Harding Picture Library **page 8** York Archaeological Trust Picture Library **page 9** (top and bottom) Michael Holford **page 10** (top) Werner Forman Archive/Statens Historiska Museum, Stockholm, (bottom) Werner Forman Archive/Thjodminjasafn, Reykjavik, Iceland (National Museum) **page 11** Ronald Sheridan, Ancient Art & Architecture Collection **page 12** (top) Michael Holford, (bottom) David Lomax, Robert Harding Picture Library, (inset) Robert Harding Picture Library **page 13** Ronald Sheridan, Ancient Art & Architecture Collection **page 15** (top) Ronald Sheridan, Ancient Art & Architecture Collection, (bottom) Werner Forman Archive/Maritime Museum, Bergen **page 16** Lindholm Hoje, Robert Harding Picture Library **page 17** (all) Ronald Sheridan, Ancient Art & Architecture Collection **page 18** (bottom) Zefa **page 19** Ronald Sheridan, Ancient Art & Architecture Collection **page 20** T.E. Clark, The Hutchison Library, (inset) R.P. Lawrence, Frank Lane Picture Agency **page**

21 (top) The Bridgeman Art Library/Heidelberg University Library, Germany, (bottom) E. & D. Hosking, Frank Lane Picture Library **page 22** Werner Forman Archive/Statens Historiska Museet, Stockholm **page 23** (top) David Lomax, Robert Harding Picture Library, (bottom) Martyn F. Chillmaid, Robert Harding Picture Library **page 24** (top) Ronald Sheridan, Ancient Art & Architecture Collection, (bottom) Rod Salm, Planet Earth Pictures **page 25** S. McCutcheon, Frank Lane Picture Agency **page 27** (top) Philip Craven, Robert Harding Picture Library, (bottom) Ronald Sheridan, Ancient Art & Architecture Collection **page 28** (top) The Hutchison Library, (middle) MacIntyre, The Hutchison Library, (bottom) Nicholas Devore, Bruce Coleman Limited **page 29** (bottom) Michael Holford **page 30** Robert Harding Picture Library **page 31** Ronald Sheridan, Ancient Art & Architecture Collection **page 32** (top and bottom) York Archaeological Trust Picture Library **page 34** (top left) Ronald Sheridan, Ancient Art & Architecture Collection, (bottom right) Werner Forman Archive/Biblioteca Nacional, Madrid **page 35** Robert Harding Picture Library **page 36** (bottom) Robert Harding Picture Library **page 37** (top) Ronald Sheridan, Ancient Art & Architecture Collection, (bottom) Anderson, Archivi Alinari **page 38** The Bridgeman Art Library/Biblioteca Medicea-Laurenziana, Florence **page 39** The Bridgeman Art Library/British Library **page 40** (top) S. Jonasson, Frank Lane Picture Agency, (middle) John Lythgoe, Planet Earth Pictures, (bottom) James D. Watt, Planet Earth Pictures **page 41** (left) Ian Yeomans, Brendan Archive, (right) Nathan Benn, Brendan Archive **page 43** Beidecke Rare Book and Manuscript Library, Yale University **page 44** Werner Forman Archive

Contents

Introduction

A Viking warrior's helmet, which gave good protection around the eyes and over the nose.

"From the fury of the Northmen, O Lord, deliver us." So prayed the people of Europe as the Vikings moved out from their homelands terrorizing those who lived in their path.

Viking is the name we give to the inhabitants of Denmark, Norway, and Sweden during the years from about A.D.750 to A.D.1100. Thanks to their activities as pirates and raiders, the Vikings have had a very bad reputation. The monks who wrote accounts of the murders and robberies committed by the men of the North could hardly be expected to write about the many Norsemen (Northmen) who stayed peacefully at home, farming, fishing, and crafting wood, metal, and ivory. Above all, it was difficult for them to give the Vikings credit for their bravery and their expertise as sailors, because it was these very qualities that enabled them to descend – like fiends out of hell – on the rest of Europe.

In winter, a favorite Viking pastime was playing board games around the fire.

Why sail into the unknown?

It is generally agreed that it was a large growth in population that caused the explosion of the Norsemen from their homelands. Some went as traders, seeking new markets for furs, amber, ivory, and other products of the North. Others set out to make their fortunes at sword point at the expense of their rich neighbors. However, because there was no longer enough fertile land to go around at home, many men and women decided to migrate to seek new homes, farms, and a better life abroad, even if it meant killing the owners to get them.

In this book, we are more concerned with the Viking farmers, traders, and colonists than with the pirates, but it is not always possible to separate them. A failed merchant or colonist could easily turn to piracy. In particular, we shall focus on the career of Eric Thorvaldsson, called Eric the Red, and his remarkable family, who earned themselves a unique place in the history of exploration. They founded the first European colony in Greenland and landed in America nearly 500 years before Columbus crossed the Atlantic!

How do we know? Archaeology has revealed a great deal about the everyday life of the Vikings, both at home and abroad. We can expect our knowledge to grow as more excavations are

A richly decorated Viking sword. The best swords were given names and passed down through the family.

Archaeology can tell us a great deal about the Vikings. The findings from this dig, one of the most useful so far, can be seen in the Jorvik Viking Centre in York, England.

Horizons

After reading this book, you may want to find out more about Eric the Red and the Vikings. At the end of some of the chapters you will find **Horizons** boxes. These boxes list some of the important people, places, ideas, and objects that are not described in this book, but which were in any case part of the Viking world. By looking up these words in the index of other reference books, you will be able to discover more about the Viking age.

conducted. Written documents are, of course, very valuable evidence, but they have certain drawbacks. Much of our written sources about the Vikings are the work of their victims, who were hardly likely to give an unbiased account. Large numbers were written many years after the events they describe, so memories had become blurred. In addition, a change of religious commitment from Odin (the most important Norse god) to Christ tended to distort the story somewhat.

The sagas

The Vikings did have a system of writing, the runes (see page 24), but they did not write books and chronicles, as did their Christian contemporaries. Instead their history and the record of the deeds of heroes were all passed from generation to generation in the form of spoken stories known as sagas.

In the 13th century, scholars among the by then Christian inhabitants of Iceland began collecting the sagas and writing them down. Many of the stories were now hundreds of years old. They had been told and retold over the centuries as entertainment on long winter evenings and at feasts.

Some sagas have undoubtedly been lost forever, but some have survived and they have preserved for us a literary treasure. There are historical records of the reigns of great kings. There are tales of the magical deeds of heroes of the remote past and the gods with whom they came into contact. Then there are the stories of real but non-royal people like Eric the Red and his family. The two sagas that tell of Eric and his migrations to Iceland and Greenland and of his children's journeys to America are to be found in Eric's Saga and the Greenlanders' Saga. Much of the detail in this book comes from these sagas.

Enter the Vikings

Muslim pilgrims at prayer around the Kaaba, the holiest shrine of Islam which stands in the mosque at Mecca

A statue of King Stephen, who was later made a saint, in Hungary

The map of Europe is redrawn

The final collapse of the Roman Empire in A.D.476 destroyed the unity of Europe. The barbarian tribes that had flooded across the frontiers set up kingdoms of their own. The Christian Church then began the slow, painful job of converting them – a process that was not completed for several hundred years. Just as the Christian missionaries had begun to make progress, Europe was faced with three new formidable enemies – the Arabs, the Magyars, and the Vikings.

The Arabs, inspired by their new faith of Islam, conquered a huge empire that stretched from the boundaries of India, across the Middle East and North Africa, into Spain and southern France. The Muslims (the followers of Islam) began to quarrel among themselves within a few years of the death of their prophet, Mohammed. Religious and political differences led to the formation of two religious parties – the Sunni and the Shi'ites – and the empire was divided between several rival royal families.

Central Europe was disrupted in the 9th century by the arrival of the Magyars, nomad tribes of horsemen from the East. These tribes settled in what we now call Hungary and proceeded to raid their new neighbors – the Franks, the Italians, and the Byzantines. These activities ended after their defeat in battle in 955 and eventually they were converted to Christianity, under King Stephen.

To many Europeans, however, the Vikings must have been the most frightening of all the menaces because of the speed and ferocity with which they struck. Their sleek dragon ships (see page 15) loomed up in the morning mist on beaches or river-banks, farther inland than their unfortunate victims had thought possible, bringing death and destruction.

Who was who

So who were they, these dreaded Vikings whose very name sent warriors to reach for their swords, priests to say their prayers, and peasants to hide in the woods with all the valuables they could carry?

They came from the area of Europe that we now call Scandinavia. They had never been part of the Roman Empire, but they had traded with it and acquired a taste for the luxury items it

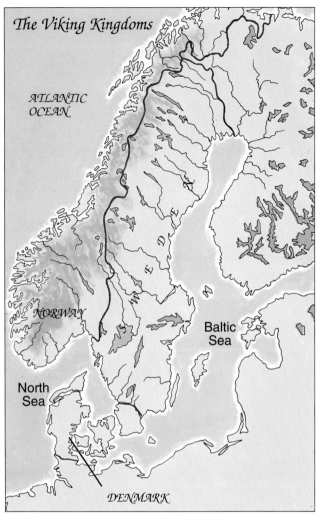

The Viking Kingdoms

ATLANTIC OCEAN

NORWAY

SWEDEN

Baltic Sea

North Sea

DENMARK

had to offer. Life went on after its collapse with far less upheaval than in the rest of Europe. Indeed the people of the North prospered and the population increased steadily.

Viking society was divided into three classes. First and foremost came the rulers – kings and great chieftains – and the warriors who served them. They looked to the great Norse god Odin for protection.

In the second, and by far the largest, class in Viking society were the free men and women. Some were landowners or tenants. Others were landless farm workers, servants, merchants, or craftsmen. Their free status gave them the right to carry arms and they were expected to be able to fight if necessary. They looked to the god Thor as their protector.

Last, and very much least, were the unfree, the thralls. Many people were born into slavery, but freemen could be reduced to slavery as a punishment for crime. No god was expected to take responsibility for such lowly folk.

In early times Scandinavia was divided into several kingdoms and the boundaries were constantly shifting. By the early 10th century, however, the kingdoms of Denmark, Norway, and Sweden were established and the kings began asserting authority over their subjects. Some chieftains and freemen found the increasing royal interference in their affairs just too much to swallow. Some turned to raiding or trading to satisfy their love of adventure and profit and to get themselves away from home. Others sought to escape completely by emigrating.

A view of Norway as the Vikings would have known it, with mountains, water, and narrow strips of fertile land.

Life at home

In Norway the sea cuts deep into the rugged coastline, forming fjords and breaking up the land. There are also mountain ranges, so fertile land is limited and cross-country travel is difficult. In Sweden, too, the amount of farmland was limited and there were great stretches of forest and many lakes. Only in Denmark was there a good supply of relatively flat land suitable for farming. But the country consisted not only of the main peninsula, attached to the European mainland, but also many islands and (at one time) southern Sweden too.

Most Vikings were farmers who lived in isolated farmhouses or small villages. Their houses were usually made of timber, but if timber was scarce, as in some of the lands they colonized, then they would also make use of stone. The houses were mostly rectangular in shape, but some might have walls that curved out slightly, so they resembled a boat. A poor man's dwelling would have one room only, with perhaps a partition at one end for the animals. A rich farmer or chief would have a large hall where his family, his warriors, servants, and slaves lived. There might also be a room or two at either end where the owner and his family had some privacy. A dwelling of that size would also have cow barns and other outbuildings around.

A farm or a village would expect to be largely self-sufficient. The Vikings grew most of their own food – oats, barley, rye, and (where possible) wheat, together with vegetables and fruit. They gathered berries and nuts and raised cattle, sheep, goats, pigs, and horses. They also kept geese, chickens, and bees. They caught fish, from both fresh water and the sea, and on northern coasts they hunted seals, walruses, and even whales. Colonies of seabirds were raided, not only for the birds themselves but also for their eggs and their feathers. The men also hunted deer and wild boars and got furs by trapping. The women wove the cloth needed for clothes and the colorful hangings used to decorate a rich man's hall. A local carpenter, smith, potter, and leatherworker

Travel on Land

Because of the nature of the Scandinavian countryside, with the islands of Denmark, the fjords and mountains of Norway, and the dense woodland and many lakes of Sweden, Vikings preferred to travel by boat on sea, river, and lake. Sometimes, however, they had to go overland. The poor had to walk, but the rich rode on horseback. Goods were carried on men's shoulders or on packhorses. Some people and goods, however, might be carried in carts. To help travelers, some rich men and women built bridges over streams in their area.

To overcome the ice and snow of winter, Viking travelers on land had several alternatives. They had skates made of bone, skis of wood, and wooden sledges that could be drawn by horses.

A leather shoe on a bone ice skate.

would, among them, make virtually everything else that was needed – tools, furniture, weapons, cooking utensils, even items for personal adornment.

However, the Vikings had to depend on traveling merchants to supply the salt used to preserve meat and fish over the winter.

Those who could afford expensive items, such as high quality weapons, and jewelry of silver and gold, would buy from merchants or skilled crafts workers in towns. Some might even be able to pay for such luxuries as silk cloth from the Far East.

The clothes worn by the people of the North were simple and practical. They were made of woolen or linen cloth, varying in quality according to wealth. Bands of embroidery were used to decorate their clothes. The men wore a tunic and trousers over a shirt. The trousers normally fitted fairly close to the leg, but those who had traveled extensively in the East sometimes wore very full breeches that ballooned out from the waist to the knee.

Women wore long dresses, over which they placed two rectangular pieces of cloth held in place by shoulder straps fastened by brooches. Over this, it later became fashionable to wear a shawl. Married women might also wear a headcloth.

Outdoors, large cloaks would be worn by both men and women. These were lined with fur against the cold, if the wearer could afford it.

Broken pieces of pottery and other household objects provide archaeologists with important clues about how people used to live. The Vikings used pots for cooking, for making beer, and for storing food.

Of gods, giants, elves, and dwarfs

The Vikings worshipped many gods and goddesses, who cared for every aspect of their daily lives in this world and the next. The ruler of the gods was Odin, the One-Eyed. He had sacrificed one of his eyes in exchange for wisdom. He was god of war, wisdom, and poetry and a rather forbidding figure. More popular and approachable was Thor, god of thunder, who kept the giants at bay with his magic hammer. Njord was ruler of the sea and the wind, while his son Freyr made the crops grow. Among the favorite goddesses were Frigg, wife of Odin, Freyja the goddess of love, and Idun, whose golden apples kept the gods forever young.

Viking brooches for a woman's dress.

Part of a 12th-century tapestry from Sweden, showing three Viking gods: Odin (far left), Thor, and Freyr.

This pendant shows Thor's magic hammer, in the shape of a cross – a sign that the pagan Vikings were being converted to Christianity.

The "light" elves were inclined to help people, if offerings were left to them, but the "dark" elves and the dwarfs were surly and not friendly to people. Dwarfs lived under the ground, working as smiths, and were generally feared by humans.

Certain hillsides, groves of trees, and rivers were all regarded as sacred places where sacrifices were made to the gods. Sacrifices were usually animals and valued objects, such as weapons and treasure, but at great festivals men were also sacrificed.

The nine worlds

The Vikings believed that there were nine worlds, which were held together by the magic ash tree called Yggdrasill. The top three worlds belonged to the gods and the light (good) elves. Warriors believed that, if they died bravely in battle, Odin's handmaidens, the Valkyries, would carry them off to Valhalla, Odin's hall, where they would live forever, feasting and practicing their battle skills.

The middle worlds belonged to humans, giants, dark (bad) elves, and dwarfs. At the bottom were the worlds of the dead, ruled over by the goddess Hel, who was part beautiful woman, part rotting corpse. At best her kingdom seems to have been a pretty gloomy place and one part appears to have been a hell of ice where evil people paid for their crimes.

The Vikings believed that one day in the future a series of natural catastrophes and ferocious wars would mark the beginning of Ragnarok — the end of the world. Gods, aided by the warriors from Valhalla, would have to fight the giants and some unpleasant monsters. Almost all would die, but a few gods would survive and they would begin again, ruled by Odin's son Balder. A man and a woman would also survive and from them a new human race would be born, to live in the new world, enjoying a golden age.

Missionaries began going to the lands of the Norsemen as early as the 8th century, but they met with little success and were likely to end up dead or enslaved. Nothing daunted, more went, but won few converts until, sometime about 960, King Harald

"Bluetooth" of Denmark was baptized. From then on Christianity spread through the Danish kingdom. The same thing happened in Norway and Sweden – once the king was baptized, his subjects followed suit. This does not mean, however, that all were enthusiastic converts and it was many years before the old gods were entirely forgotten.

Have sword, will travel

The most important single factor that drove men abroad, as raiders or colonists, was a shortage of land at home. The population had been steadily increasing over a long period. More and more land was brought under cultivation until, certainly in Norway and Sweden, all the reasonable farmland was occupied. Younger sons therefore had to make their own way in the world. They were very likely to join a chieftain who was looking for good men to go on a raid to a rich, poorly defended country (such as England during the reign of King Ethelred the Unready). If, however, they were farmers at heart and wanted to settle down, they would join forces with others who felt the same and seek their fortune abroad in familiar areas of Europe or beyond the known horizons, even though they knew they would almost certainly have to fight for their new homes.

An 11th-century image of a Viking warrior, carved in deer antler.

Horizons

Other peoples who were on the move seeking new homes, besides the Vikings, included the Khazars, who moved from Central Asia to southern Russia; the Seljuk Turks; the Patzinaks who moved from Central Asia into the Balkans; and the Bulgars, who also settled in the Balkans.

Words Left Behind

Even today there are a few clues that tell us where the Vikings settled, particularly in Britain. These clues are in the names of English villages and towns.

thorpe – at the end of a place name means *village*
thwaite – means *meadow*
by – means *farm*
gate – means *street*

The English city of York was called **Jorvik** by the Vikings. There are several ideas about the origin of the word **Viking**. It may come from **vik**, meaning a bay or fjord (in a place where a pirate might hide!). It may come from the Norse words for a pirate, a robber, raiding, or warfare at sea.

Vikings Rule the Waves

The Vikings carved memorial stones to dead warriors. The pictures tell us about their ships, clothes, battles, and much more.

The Osberg ship (below, reconstructed and inset, a replica) was excavated at Oseberg in Norway. It was probably used as the burial ship for a Norwegian queen.

The boat builders

The men of Scandinavia had been building boats for centuries. Pictures on rocks and carved stones, together with the remains of actual ships, give us an excellent idea of what these vessels looked like, the way they were built, and how well they would perform at sea. It is most unusual to find remains of actual ships, but a few have been saved from the rapid decay that is the normal fate of objects made of wood. They have survived either because they were buried in graves where the soil conditions happened to be just right to preserve them, or because they were sunk in the sea, again under conditions ideal to preserve them.

As boat builders and as sailors, the Norsemen were the best of their day. Only Alfred the Great of England managed to challenge them at sea for a short while, with a special built-to-order fleet.

Viking ships had a keel, the ship's backbone, and were clinker-built, that is with the strakes (planks) overlapping one another.

Alfred the Great

In the 9th century, England was in crisis with a large Danish Viking army occupying the kingdoms of East Anglia and Northumbria, so in 871 the Kingdom of Wessex chose Alfred, the only adult male member of the royal house, as king. Alfred was an extraordinary man, the only king to whom the English have awarded the name "great." In a seemingly hopeless position, he hung on grimly, not only reorganizing his army and inspiring the men to fight the Danes, but also building burghs, towns with defenses where ordinary people could shelter in time of danger. He even beat the Danes at their own game by building large ships and successfully challenging their command of the sea. During the next 80 years, his descendants advanced, steadily gaining victories over the Danes till the whole of England was united under their rule. Then came the deplorable king Ethelred and Vikings flocked to England again, eager to help him live up to his nickname – Unready, meaning without good advice.

The strakes were caulked with wool soaked in tar to make them watertight and were fastened together with iron rivets. The tenth strake up from the keel had to be especially strong as it was on the waterline. So did the fourteenth, because it had the holes for the oars. The ribs, which were tied to the strakes, were only put in once the tenth strake was in position. The best ships were made of carefully chosen timber, probably oak, and were light, strong, and flexible. All these features were very important, particularly in voyages through eastern Europe (see page 19). Here the Vikings sailed as far as possible up the rivers that flowed into the Baltic, then lifted the ships out of the water and carried them overland to the next river.

The square sails were mostly made of woolen cloth and might be plain bright colors or striped. When in full sail, there would be considerable strain on the mast, so precautions were taken to hold it firmly in place and to avoid the hull being damaged. The bottom of the mast was mounted in a heavy block of wood called a kerling. This in turn rested on the keel but was fastened to the ribs. In this way the weight was evenly distributed over the center section of the ship. A large piece of wood called the mast fish (because of its shape) and the mast lock held the mast firmly in position.

The longships

The Vikings' fighting ships are called longships or dragon ships. Both names describe them accurately. They were long and sleek, fast and easy to maneuver. They were propelled by sail or oars, according to weather conditions, and, when at sea, they bore the carved head of a fierce dragon on the prow. The carving was removed in harbor because it was believed that some of the bad spirits of the land would be angered by the presence of a dragon.

The seating arrangements on board these longships are uncertain. No benches for the rowers have yet been found, so they may have sat on the sea chests, in which they stowed their belongings. The smallest size dragon ship probably held 26 oars (13 on each side). However 16 to 20 per side was probably standard. We know of some royal flagships that were enormous, with up to 35 oars on each side.

Merchant ships

In contrast to the longships of the warriors, merchants (and, of course, colonists) preferred ships that were not so long, but much wider. The extra width allowed merchants to carry cargo and colonists to transport their farm animals and the seeds for future crops. Adequate supplies of food and water for long voyages could also be carried. These ships, called knorrs, were propelled by sail only.

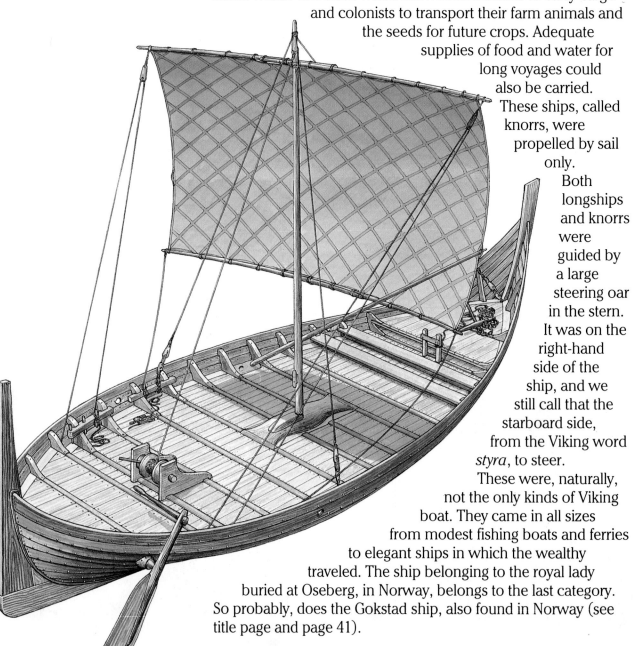

Both longships and knorrs were guided by a large steering oar in the stern. It was on the right-hand side of the ship, and we still call that the starboard side, from the Viking word *styra*, to steer.

These were, naturally, not the only kinds of Viking boat. They came in all sizes from modest fishing boats and ferries to elegant ships in which the wealthy traveled. The ship belonging to the royal lady buried at Oseberg, in Norway, belongs to the last category. So probably, does the Gokstad ship, also found in Norway (see title page and page 41).

A Viking longship

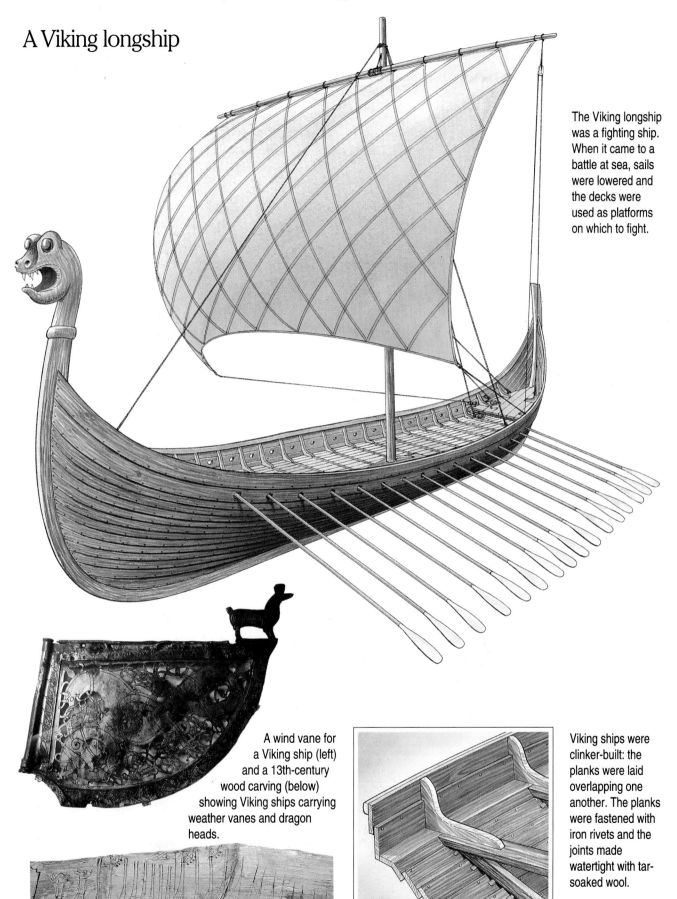

The Viking longship was a fighting ship. When it came to a battle at sea, sails were lowered and the decks were used as platforms on which to fight.

A wind vane for a Viking ship (left) and a 13th-century wood carving (below) showing Viking ships carrying weather vanes and dragon heads.

Viking ships were clinker-built: the planks were laid overlapping one another. The planks were fastened with iron rivets and the joints made watertight with tar-soaked wool.

Navigational skills

Some people have credited the Vikings with inventing various ingenious navigational instruments. The evidence, however, is very sparse and should be treated with great caution. There is, for example, a small piece of wood, which was found in Greenland. It has been reconstructed as a dial with compass points marked on it and it is suggested that it was used to check a ship's direction against the sun or stars. While not impossible, it was really unnecessary. In the early days ships very rarely strayed out of sight of the coasts. When they did begin to venture across stretches of open sea there were doubtless many ships lost at first. However, there were very skilled and experienced navigators available. They had learned to judge time and speed and determine their position from the sun and stars. They had also become experts in the ways of seabirds and mammals, weather, tides, and wave formations. From observing such things, they could draw conclusions about weather conditions and where land was likely to lie.

Boat Burials

In pagan Scandinavia, royalty and very rich chiefs were often buried in boats. The dead person was splendidly dressed and surrounded with all his or her personal possessions and the equipment that would be needed in the next world. A personal slave and the deceased's favorite horses and dogs would be sacrificed and sent along too. Some of these death ships may have been set on fire and then pushed out to drift on the waves. Others were definitely burned on land, like the one described by the Arab traveler Ibn Fadlan. A mound would then be raised over the ashes. Other ships and their contents were buried intact in pits with a mound of earth thrown up over them. Occasionally, if soil conditions were right and the graves were not attacked by robbers, the ships and their contents have been reasonably preserved. They give us a wonderful insight into the Viking way of life and the skills of their craftsmen. Families who could not afford to sacrifice a perfectly good boat in a grave might nevertheless bury a dead relative under part of a boat (presumably, an old, wrecked one) or in a boat-shaped grave outlined with stones.

Some Vikings were buried in boat-shaped graves, outlined with stones. This one is in Denmark.

Outrage

It was toward the end of the 8th century that the first Viking raids shook Europe. From Scotland in the north to the Mediterranean world in the south, no one was prepared for such attacks, let alone their speed and ferocity. The raiders had it easy and the pickings were rich. The trickle of Viking ships became a flood.

They came in summer, at first in small numbers – say three or four ships sailing together. They would run their shallow-draft ships up on a beach or sail up rivers. Thanks to their shallow draft, the ships could reach amazingly far inland. There would be a wild rush ashore, looting, killing, and burning. No one was spared, unless they would be useful to sell as slaves. Good-looking young women and children were most in demand. Monasteries were sacked along with villages. Priests were killed as well as peasants. If the raid was a success and there was no likelihood of reprisals from a local lord and his warband, the raiders might have a feast to celebrate. They would gorge on the slaughtered animals, drink up all the local wine and ale, and rape any female prisoners. They might range the countryside for a day or two on horses they had stolen, looting as they went. But soon they would move on, repeat the performance a time or two, and then sail back home with their booty and slaves, if any, before the autumn gales.

The rich, often weak and divided kingdoms of Europe were easy prey for the Viking hunters. They presented a target too tempting to resist. A few great monarchs such as Charlemagne, king of the Franks, and Alfred, king of England (see page 13), managed to hold the Norsemen at bay for a while. Others were either distracted by struggles with their own people or they lacked the courage to face what appeared to be an invincible enemy. In fairness, most also lacked the skill and the resources to defeat the sea wolves. They could not guard every inch of coast or every river mouth. They did not have enough men. Some fought and lost. Many preferred to buy off the Vikings with Danegeld – large bribes in money raised from taxes. But that bought only temporary relief. The Vikings accepted the silver and gold happily, went home, and boasted of their luck. Soon more Vikings would descend, demanding larger and larger ransoms.

Take-over

In some areas – Spain, southern France, and Italy, for example – the Vikings did no more than raid. Elsewhere, however, they took note of the rich and fertile lands they were looting and decided to stay. They began to spend winters in the lands of their victims, building fortified camps as bases. From these they spread out, occupying the adjacent countryside, and forcing the local inhabitants to flee or submit to their rule. Sometimes they came to an arrangement with a local monarch, allowing them to settle. In France, for example, in 911, King Charles "the Simple" came to an agreement with a

This beautifully decorated book is one of the few to survive the Viking raids in England. Many were simply burned by the invaders.

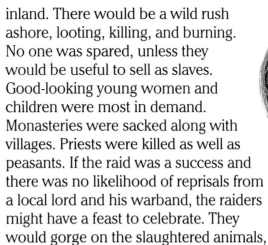
This 7th-century Anglo-Saxon brooch shows the kind of wealth that attracted the Viking raiders to foreign shores.

Charlemagne was one of the first monarchs in Europe to use mounted troops to fight the Vikings.

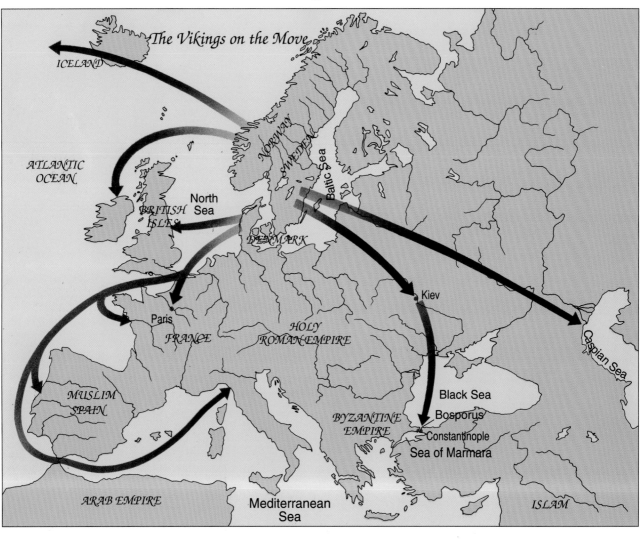

The Vikings on the Move

ICELAND

ATLANTIC OCEAN

NORWAY

SWEDEN

Baltic Sea

North Sea

BRITISH ISLES

DENMARK

Kiev

Paris

FRANCE

HOLY ROMAN EMPIRE

Caspian Sea

MUSLIM SPAIN

Black Sea

Bosporus

BYZANTINE EMPIRE

Constantinople

Sea of Marmara

ARAB EMPIRE

Mediterranean Sea

ISLAM

The fertile countryside of Normandy must have delighted the Viking settlers.

group of Vikings led by a chief called Rollo. They were given a province in northern France in which to settle (in fact they already occupied it), in return for defending it against other Viking raiders! The province became known as Northmen's land – Normandy – and, having been baptized, Rollo became its duke. His descendant William was the conqueror who defeated the Anglo-Saxons at Hastings in 1066. Once established, Rollo's warriors sent for their families and they went back to being farmers and traders, fighting only if the need arose.

It would be wrong to suggest that the Danes, Norwegians, and Swedes always operated separately, in specific areas. A large fleet was likely to contain men from all over Scandinavia. However, generally speaking, it was the Danes who mostly concentrated on England, Wales, Ireland, France, and the Mediterranean world, and the Norwegians who went to Scotland, Iceland, and farther west. Swedish activity centered on the lands around the eastern Baltic. Their settlements there acted as a springboard to the territories of the Slavs, where a Swedish Viking called Rurik and his family carved out a kingdom for themselves. The Slavs called their unwelcome new overlords "Rus," so the area where they settled eventually became Russia. From this base they moved south and east on trading expeditions. These journeys took them as far south as the great city of Constantinople and as far east as the Caspian Sea and even Baghdad.

Working for the emperor

When the western half of the Roman Empire fell to the barbarians (see page 6), the eastern part, with its capital at Constantinople, survived as the Byzantine Empire. When the Vikings reached Constantinople, which they called Miklagard ("the Great City"), they were most impressed and were eager to buy the luxury goods to be obtained there. Soon, however, the Rus princes began to look on Miklagard with greedy eyes as one more city to be captured and plundered. They made several determined assaults on the city, sending their fleets down the rivers, into the Black Sea, and so to the Bosporus, a strait that connects the Black Sea and the Sea of Marmara. In a straight sea fight, the Byzantines would probably have lost to the Vikings, but the wily Byzantines had a secret weapon, a mixture of chemicals that burned fiercely on water. It devastated the Viking fleets, time after time.

This mosaic is a fragment of the decoration the Vikings might have seen in a Christian church in Constantinople. Much of the splendor of the church was destroyed when it was taken by the Turks in 1453 and converted to a mosque.

Finally, in 988 Vladimir, prince of Kiev, one of the Rus princes, decided it was better to cooperate and trade with the Byzantines than to make futile attempts to conquer them. So he sent warriors to help the Byzantine emperor in his wars. Individual Vikings had already served previous emperors as mercenaries, but Vladimir sent a force of 6,000 men. The emperor was not slow to appreciate the fighting qualities of the Vikings and soon found they had one additional quality – they were loyal to the man who paid them. This was more than could be said for many of the emperor's own subjects! From Vladimir's force grew an imperial bodyguard called the Varangian ("sword men") Guard. Rus and Vikings from Scandinavia served successive emperors in the Varangian Guard and, after their defeat at Hastings, many Anglo-Saxons joined, too.

Go West, Young Man

Had the men of Scandinavia simply launched themselves westward across the unknown waters of the North Atlantic, they would have faced a terrible journey, without any guarantee that there was land at the end of it. Even if there was, they might not find it. But, of course, it was not quite like that.

The island-hoppers

Vikings, particularly from Norway, raided Scotland at the end of the 8th century. Their route must have taken them by way of the Shetland and Orkney islands. Indeed, with a good wind the journey to Shetland from Norway's west coast could take as little as 24 hours. They progressed from these islands to the mainland and to the other islands, including the Hebrides and on to the Faeroes. Norwegians settled in the Scottish islands, as well as on the mainland, finding conditions not unlike those that they were used to at home.

The discovery of the islands around the coasts of Scotland and then Ireland was the key to the Vikings' expansion westward. However, as it happened, they were not the first to sail west. Ironically, they were following in the wake of small groups of brave Irish monks, who were seeking the solitude they believed they needed to draw them close to God. These unlikely explorers had already sailed their small skin-covered boats from island to island and had reached the Faeroes by about 700.

Thule

The Greek explorer Pytheas of Marseilles made the first known circumnavigation of

This upturned boat is similar to those used by Irish monks hundreds of years ago. Skins were used to cover a frame (inset, the frame of a small coracle).

This medieval manuscript shows one of the hazards the monks believed they would have to face on the voyages in unknown waters.

Britain about 300 B.C. before straying even farther north. Thanks to his voyages, early geographers were aware of the existence of an island, which they said was far away, near the frozen wastes on the very edge of the world. They called it Thule; we know it better as Iceland.

A book on geography, written in 825 by an Irish scholar, shows that a few Irish monks (perhaps seeking to get away from the Vikings who settled in the Faeroes in the early 9th century) had braved the unknown waters of the west and reached Iceland. They were not left in peace for long.

Sometime between 860 and 870, three different Viking ships visited Iceland. Soon after this, Viking settlers began to arrive there. Some of the newcomers may have been seeking to escape the control of the king of Norway. Many others were simply looking for farmland and by about 930, all the usable land in Iceland had been occupied. The fate of the Irish monks is unknown.

Most of the colonists were Norwegians, coming from Norway itself, or from Norwegian settlements in the Scottish islands, and from Ireland. Some of these Norwegian settlers had married Celtic women and owned Irish slaves too, so a little Celtic blood was also represented on Iceland.

Iceland must have looked much like this when the Vikings first landed there.

Crime and Punishment

When a freeman like Eric was accused of a crime, his accusers hauled him up before their local Thing. A Thing was a meeting of all the freemen of a district, probably held once a year, to decide local policies and laws and to judge those who had broken them.

Having no jails where criminals could be confined, punishments had to be more immediate. A persistent troublemaker, as Eric clearly was, might be declared an outlaw. A sentence of outlawry was almost the same as banishment because the man was literally outside the law and the protection that it offered. Anyone could kill him without fear of punishment. So it was best if the outlaw fled beyond the reach of all who knew him.

Under Viking law, the life of every person was thought to have a money value. It was called a wergild. If a person was slain, the murderer had to pay the wergild to his victim's relatives. Naturally the wergild for, say, a rich farmer was far higher than that for a landless old servant. Failure to pay would lead to outlawry. That way, people were discouraged from taking the law into their own hands and killing the killer, which could lead to a feud between the two families.

These early Viking coins, showing longships, were probably minted in Denmark but they were found in the Viking market-place at Birka, in Sweden.

Gunnbjarnar Skerries

About the year 900, a man called Gunnbjorn was in command of a ship sailing from Norway to Iceland, when it was hit by bad weather and blown off course. He sighted the coast of another island, which was later named for him – Gunnbjarnar Skerries. Gunnbjorn managed to reach Iceland and reported the sighting, but no one was particularly interested. A few years later, however, when no more land was to be had in Iceland, a group of Vikings decided to try their luck on Gunnbjarnar Skerries. They left Iceland in 978 but the settlement failed totally. Following a winter of intense cold and violent quarrels that ended in murder, the survivors limped back to Iceland.

Enter Eric the Red

Eric, called Eric the Red, son of Thorvald Asvaldsson, was not a man to be crossed without good reason. His red hair and beard earned him his nickname, but his fiery temper may have had something to do with it as well. He and his father had to leave their home in Norway in a hurry "because of some killings." They went to Iceland and settled at a place called Drangar, and it was there that Thorvald died. Eric married a woman called Thjodhild and moved south, clearing land for his new homestead. Before long, however, he was in trouble again. He was involved in a feud, in which he killed two men. For this Eric was outlawed and so he set up again in yet another area. Once more Eric's hasty temper landed him in the thick of a feud, during which several men died. In 982 the local Thing outlawed him.

When Eric was outlawed, he and his men set sail for the island of Gunnbjarnar Skerries. They landed on the east coast, near a glacier they named Blueshirt. Leaving this unpromising area they sailed south, and entered warmer waters on the southwest side of the island. They spent three years there. Each summer they went off exploring again. In the summer of the third year they returned to Iceland. Even then Eric could not keep out of trouble. While persuading people to emigrate to the land he had explored, he got into a fight with an old enemy and friends had to help to patch up a peace.

A fjord in southwest Greenland (above), similar to the site Eric chose for his farmstead, and (right) a turf house in Iceland which shows the kind of building construction that the Greenland settlers would have used.

Greenland

When Eric spoke of his discoveries to would-be settlers, he renamed the new country Greenland. He thought that people would be more tempted to go there if it had an attractive name. Twenty-five ships set off with him the following year (986) but only 14 reached their destination. Some were lost at sea, others returned to Iceland.

Though much of Greenland is covered with snow and ice, the southern tip is actually farther south than Iceland, on the same line of latitude as the Shetlands. Moreover, at that time, the climate was going through a phase when the weather was slightly warmer than it is now. The new arrivals were able to farm the land at this end of the island. Greenland, unlike Iceland, already had a native population – Eskimos. However they were found much farther north than the Norse colonists, and they lived by seal hunting.

Eric's people settled in the southwestern corner where fjords like those in their Norwegian homeland bit into the coastline. Good pasture was to be found at the head of the fjords. Eric and his wife Thjodhild chose the best site available to build their farmstead of stone and turf, which they called Brattahlid.

Runes

An alphabetic system of writing called runes was invented in Scandinavia in the late 2nd century A.D.

There were originally 24 runes, but by about 800 they were reduced in number to 16. Unfortunately, the only inscriptions in runes to have survived are either on memorial stones (raised to the dead, giving their names and a few brief words about them) or were inscribed on objects to indicate who owned them. Either way, the inscriptions are short. There are no books about the Vikings, written by the Vikings themselves.

In the 11th century, as Scandinavia was converted to Christianity, runes were replaced by the Roman alphabet.

Runes (top two rows) carved on a wall in Orkney, Scotland.

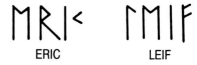

Some runes and their meaning.

The other colonists settled nearby in similar houses. This area became known as the Eastern Settlement because another group soon settled some 180 miles to the northwest and that community was called the Western Settlement. There were eventually 190 farms in the Eastern Settlement and 90 in the Western.

The good life?

Life was never easy in Greenland, but at first the colonists did well and later there were some 3,000 of them. By 1030, all the available farming land was taken. The pasture was good and they kept cattle, pigs, sheep, and goats, which they brought with them from Iceland. They may even, for a time, have grown a little barley. They hunted reindeer as well as seals, walruses, and whales and the teeming fish and countless birds that abounded in the sea and on the coasts.

Stunted willow and birch trees grew at the head of the fjords and there were quantities of driftwood to be gathered for fires. However the settlers had to import most of the timber and grain, and all the metals (especially iron) they needed. Of course any luxury goods they wanted had to be imported. They could pay for these goods by exporting items that were highly prized in Europe: furs (particularly of arctic fox and polar bear), the ivory tusks of walrus and narwhal, hides, and hunting falcons. They even sometimes sent live polar bears to a king for his private zoo.

The settlers were self-governing and, as in

The Viking settlers in Greenland hunted walrus and traded their ivory tusks for goods they needed from home.

Iceland, had an assembly that met annually at Gardar, making laws and dispensing justice.

They also spent considerable time and energy exploring their new homeland, even north of the Arctic Circle.

Eric and Thjodhild had three sons – Leif, Thorvald, and Thorstein – and a daughter called Freydis. Christianity came to Greenland round about 1000. According to the sagas (see page 5), Eric was against the new religion, but Thjodhild was apparently converted and she built a church at Brattahlid. It was very small, about 6.5 feet by 11.5 feet inside its thick turf walls. It was placed at a little distance from the farmstead, perhaps because of Eric's dislike of the new faith. Even Eric the Red, however, could not hold back the spread of the Christian faith, and anyway he died soon after. In 1125 Greenland got its own bishop. His stone cathedral was built at Gardar and archaeologists have since excavated 16 parish churches.

Decline and fall

When Eric died, in 1001, he left a thriving community. But the good life was not to last. The climate began to worsen in the latter part of the 13th century. It affected the whole of Europe and the bad weather was responsible for the famine that struck Europe from 1315 to 1317.

In Greenland, though the temperature only dropped a few degrees, it was enough to tip the balance against the colonists. Inland the central ice sheet began expanding, while at sea icebergs became common much farther south than ever before. The journey to Greenland had always been difficult. The icebergs made it increasingly hazardous and fewer ships arrived. This meant additional problems for those awaiting supplies of grain, timber, and iron. Food became scarce and the undernourished people and animals died in various epidemics.

The cold weather brought the Eskimo people south and into conflict with the settlers. The Western Settlement disappeared sometime in the mid-14th century. The Eastern Settlement survived for a while, but there, too, problems became acute and in 1387 they were attacked by the Eskimos. The Eastern Settlement was still in existence in 1409 but sometime after that it ceased. The fate of the occupants is uncertain. Many probably died of cold, hunger, and disease. Some were killed by Eskimos and others may even have joined up with them. Perhaps a few made it back to Iceland and a few more may have sailed west to a land also connected with Eric the Red's family.

The Eskimos were well adapted to the cold weather that brought the Viking settlements in Greenland to an end.

Vinland the Good

First sighting

One of the men who emigrated to Greenland with Eric the Red in 986 was Herjolf Bardarson. He took land in the Eastern Settlement and built a farm called Herjolfsness. Herjolf had a son, Bjarni, who did not manage to sail at the same time as the main group, but set out slightly later. He had bad luck with the weather and lost his way in gales and fog. When conditions cleared a bit he saw, to the southwest, the hills and forests of some unknown shore. Bjarni realized he was too far off course for this to be Greenland, so he sailed to the north and sighted land again. This land could not be his destination either, for it was also wooded, but low-lying. Off he sailed again, northward, and this time he reached a coast with mountains and glaciers. This still did not meet the description Eric had given him of Greenland, so he tried again. Four days later, a gale-force wind carried him not only to Greenland, but to Herjolfsness itself, where he was reunited with his father. Bjarni told people of his adventure, then settled down to the life of a farmer, eventually inheriting Herjolfsness. The unknown lands were of no interest to him any more, except as a good story to be told around the fire on a winter's evening.

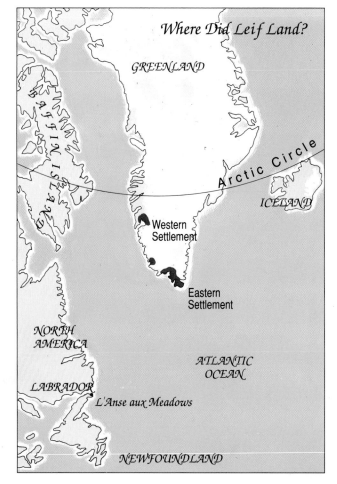

Where Did Leif Land?

GREENLAND

BAFFIN ISLAND

Arctic Circle

ICELAND

Western Settlement

Eastern Settlement

NORTH AMERICA

ATLANTIC OCEAN

LABRADOR

L'Anse aux Meadows

NEWFOUNDLAND

Leif the Lucky

Most people forgot about Bjarni Herjolfsson's discovery, but one young man – Eric the Red's eldest son, Leif – had paid particular attention. A few years later, about the year 1000, Leif bought Bjarni's ship and decided to retrace, as near as possible, Bjarni's course and explore the lands he had sighted.

Leif persuaded his father to go with him, but, just before departure, Eric fell heavily from a horse and injured his leg, so he could not go. Leif and his sailors set out without him, sailing southwest. After a short while they reached a land of ice and rock, presumably the last of the places Bjarni had seen. Leif called it Helluland (Slab-land), and set off again till he came to the low-lying coast with forests. This he called Markland (Forest-land), and sailed south once more till he reached a most attractive stretch of coast. The climate was mild, there was grass for their cattle, and salmon to catch in the rivers. They also found grapes, which caused Leif to name it Vinland (Wine-land). Leif and his

Leif and his companions found grapes growing in Vinland, although the wild fruit he saw would have been much smaller than these modern cultivated grapes.

The Vikings had cups, but they also used drinking horns like this one with its silver rim.

companions spent the winter there and thus became the first known Europeans to set foot in America. In the spring they sailed safely home.

As they approached the Greenland coast, Leif caught sight of a reef on which survivors of a shipwreck were clinging. He rescued 15 people, including the leader, Thorir, and his wife, Gudrid. He took them home to Greenland. This act of bravery, which had meant risking his own vessel, earned Leif the name of "the Lucky." And so he seemed to be for, from then on, we are told, he gained greatly in wealth and reputation.

Eric the Red died the winter after his son's safe return.

Where was Vinland?

Just exactly where were the places visited by Leif and his family? Opinions differ, especially over the location of Vinland itself.

Helluland, with its rocky landscape, is generally thought to be Baffin Island, just across the Davis Strait from Greenland, but the northern coast of Labrador is a possibility. Markland and its low-lying forests are generally placed in southern Labrador. Vinland is the real problem. It was south of Markland, but how far south? Locations have been suggested from Newfoundland, through New England to Florida. There is even some disagreement over the meaning of the name. Does "Vin" refer to grapes and wine,

Baffin Island is thought to be Leif's Helluland.

Labrador fits Leif's description of Markland.

Leif's Vinland may have been somewhere on the Newfoundland coast.

as most people say? Or does it, as some scholars argue, refer to grass, which is another meaning of the word?

On the whole, the balance of opinion favors the Newfoundland/New England area, though we may never know for sure. Between 1960 and 1968 excavations were carried out at a site in Newfoundland called L'Anse aux Meadows (its original name was L'Anse aux Méduse, Jellyfish Creek). The foundations of buildings were discovered that resembled those found in the Viking settlements in Greenland. Also small items identified as Viking were found. Carbon-14 tests gave an 11th-century date. So, it was a Viking settlement, but was it the one built by Leif and his family? That we cannot know without a written inscription, and we are not likely to get one. There must have been other visitors to Vinland besides Leif and his family. We know about Leif only because of the survival of Eric's Saga and the Greenlanders' Saga. If sagas were composed about the others, they have not survived. More likely it was only Eric and his family that deserved sagas of their own because they were the first in Greenland and Vinland and probably because they were such colorful characters.

How Thorvald Ericsson found a home

During the winter after his return, Leif was closely questioned about Vinland by his brother Thorvald. In the spring Thorvald gathered a crew of 30 and, using Leif's ship, set off to explore

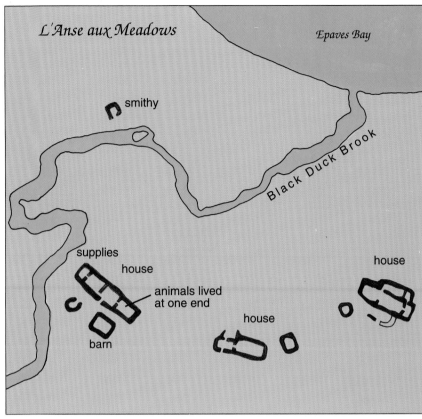

L'Anse aux Meadows

Epaves Bay

smithy

Black Duck Brook

supplies
house

animals lived
at one end

barn

house

house

house

A plan of the Viking site excavated in Newfoundland.

This is a 16th-century painting, but the Native Americans in it may look like those who traded, and then fought, with the Vikings. The boats are certainly like those in the story.

Vinland further. They found the houses Leif had built and settled down for the winter, catching fish for their food. In the spring, while the main party was getting their ship ready, some took the ship's boat and sailed on, exploring the coast. They found it a very pleasant land but saw no people. When the party was reunited, they set off for home but were driven ashore in a fierce gale. They had to spend some time repairing damage to the ship's keel. Then they sailed once more and found themselves at a promontory between two fjords and set out to explore. Thorvald thought the place was so beautiful that he wanted to make his home there, but when they were returning to their ship, they came across three skin boats on the sandy beach. Three men were hiding under each boat. The Norsemen killed eight of them, but one got away and went to get help. When Thorvald and his men were asleep, the natives attacked them in force. Thorvald and his men called them Skraelings, which means wretches. These "wretches" (generally assumed to be Native North Americans) proved a match for the Vikings and Thorvald received a wound from which he died. At his request, his men buried him at the place he had wanted to make his home. They spent the winter in Vinland, then sailed home to tell Leif of his brother's fate.

Meanwhile, back in Greenland, Thorstein, brother of Leif and Thorvald, had married Gudrid, whom Leif had rescued on his way back from Vinland. Gudrid's husband Thorir had fallen sick and died in Leif's home soon after their rescue. Thorstein and Gudrid set out to bring Thorvald's body back to Greenland, but bad weather forced them to put into the Western Settlement. Here Thorstein fell sick and died, leaving Gudrid a widow for a second time. She returned to Leif at Brattahlid, where she met and fell in love with a visiting captain from Norway called Thorfinn.

A replica of a Viking knorr, the kind of ship that the men and women who sailed to Vinland would have used.

Thorfinn in Vinland

There was naturally much talk about Vinland at Brattahlid and Thorfinn and Gudrid decided to go there. They gathered a company of 60 men and five women, together with livestock, because they wanted to settle there.

They found Leif's houses in Vinland without much trouble and passed an agreeable winter, without food shortages. In the summer a large group of Skraelings appeared out of the woods one day, but the settlers' bull began to bellow and the Skraelings were terrified. Although they could not understand each other's language, some sort of understanding was reached and the two sides began to trade. The Skraelings sold furs in return for woolen cloth, and for milk from the Vikings' cows.

Not trusting in the continued goodwill of the Skraelings, Thorfinn had a strong wooden palisade built around the houses. There Gudrid gave birth to a son, whom they called Snorri – the first recorded child of European origin to be born in America. The second winter saw the Skraelings return in great numbers to trade. All went well until, it is said, one of the Skraelings was caught trying to steal some weapons and was killed. The rest fled, but returned later. There was a battle, which the Vikings eventually won. According to one of the sagas, Eric's strong-minded daughter Freydis and her husband Thorvard were among Thorfinn's party. During the Skraeling attack things were going badly for the Norsemen and they were retreating. Freydis, who was pregnant, tried to rally the men. She seized a sword and prepared to fight, baring her breast and slapping it with her sword. The Skraelings were so terrified by this unusual spectacle that they fled! Freydis was much praised for her courage.

Thorfinn and his people were very lonely so far from family and friends. Obtaining food and supplies was difficult. Now that the Skraelings were also hostile he decided it was too dangerous to stay. So they gathered up the many pelts they had bought from the Skraelings and returned to Greenland. Eventually, Thorfinn and Gudrid settled in Iceland and, according to the sagas, became the ancestors of several prominent people, including three bishops.

Murder!

Freydis, daughter of Eric the Red, was a very independent woman and, one might say, a real chip off the old block. We are told she

A 10th-century axe head.

was proud and fond of money. She also had a fierce temper and was, one suspects, no Christian.

One day she called on two men, brothers, who were visiting from Iceland. She persuaded them to bring their ship and join her on an expedition to Vinland. They would all share in the profits. Whether or not she had consulted her husband, Thorvard, is unknown. In view of her later actions, probably not.

It was agreed that Freydis would take 30 men on her ship and the brothers would have the same number on theirs. From the beginning Freydis cheated. She hid five extra men on her ship, presumably because she already had a plan in mind.

No sooner had they landed than a quarrel broke out about over who should occupy Leif's old house. Freydis defied the two brothers and they and their men, together with the five women who had accompanied them, moved off and built their houses some way inland.

During the winter, bad feeling between the two camps grew worse. Then one day Freydis rose early and went to the brothers' camp. She met Finnbogi and came to an arrangement with him. If the brothers would give her their ship, which was larger than hers, she would leave and return to Greenland. Finnbogi, evidently pleased at the idea of getting rid of her so easily, readily agreed. Freydis returned home and told her husband that she had gone to try and make peace with the brothers but that they had beaten, abused, and humiliated her. Thorvard must avenge her. Goaded by her taunts, Thorvard led their men on a surprise raid. He captured the brothers and their men in their house and sent them out, one by one. Freydis was waiting outside and had them all killed. No one wanted to kill the women, however, so Freydis grabbed an axe and did the deed herself. She made everyone swear to keep silent about what had happened. They were to go home and say that the brothers and their people had decided to stay in Vinland.

In the spring Freydis and her crew returned with their cargo of timber and furs to Greenland. They made a handsome profit and all became rich. Someone, however, let the cat out of the bag. Leif was horrified when he heard what Freydis had done, but he did nothing to punish her. We are told that, after this, no one thought well of her, but she seems to have gotten away with her crimes.

With the expedition of Freydis and her partners our information about visits to, and attempts to colonize, America comes to an end. It is possible that others went, but we do not have the records. Certainly, in time, all visits stopped. It was just too far away and the Skraelings, who were probably from a North American Indian tribe, were too numerous and too hostile. Colonization at that time was simply too difficult.

Horizons

Places where interesting things were happening during the Viking Age: Central America, where the Maya civilization was in its golden age; Japan, where the Fujiwara family had power over the emperors; the Empire of Ghana; Cambodia, where the magnificent civilization of the Khmers flourished, with their capital at Angkor Wat; the Caliphate of Cordoba in Spain; Baghdad, capital of the caliphs of the Abbasid Dynasty.

Back in Europe

Viking settlers captured Jorvik (now called York), in the north of England, in A.D. 866. Life-size reconstructions at the Jorvik Viking Centre show scenes from Viking life in the 10th century, when Jorvik was a great trading port. (Below) inside a typical house, and (bottom) in the harbor.

With their conversion to Christianity, it might be thought that the Vikings would have settled down in the mainstream of European life and lost their distinctive identity. It is certainly true that those in the British Isles, France, and Russia had apparently started to conform and to be absorbed into the native populations. But the Viking spirit was far from dead.

The battle for England

When the Vikings had begun their determined attack to win lands in England in the 9th century, they had conquered parts of north, east, and central England. These areas became known collectively as the "Danelaw," because Danish laws and customs were followed, rather than Anglo-Saxon ones. In the southwest, Alfred the Great, king of Wessex, had halted the Danish advance. He insisted on their leader being converted to Christianity. He even regained some territory from them. Alfred's descendants built on his achievements and united the whole of England under their rule.

Then came the reign of Alfred's unworthy great-great-grandson Ethelred, called the Redeless. This is usually given in modern English as "Unready." But its real meaning is "devoid of counsel, or lacking advice," rather than "unprepared" – though he was that too. In his reign, many delighted Vikings flocked to his shores and collected Danegeld from him (see page 17), but the Danish king Sweyn Forkbeard saw England as ripe for conquest. In alliance with the Norwegian king he invaded in 994 and failed. Undeterred, he came back in 1003 and again in 1013. On this last occasion the men of the Danelaw transferred their allegiance to him. Ethelred fled and Sweyn was the actual ruler, but he died suddenly in 1014. Ethelred returned, only to die within two years. Ethelred's eldest son fought stubbornly to keep his throne but he was killed and Sweyn's son Canute became king of England and Denmark. Canute was a true Viking, hailed by his men as terrible in battle, a "ruthless provider of food for wolf and the raven" (meaning he killed many men). However he was also a great giver of gifts, which in Viking eyes made everything all right.

The Norman connection

Ethelred's second wife was Emma, daughter of Duke Richard I of Normandy, and so descended from the Viking Rollo (see page 18). When Canute had gained control of England, the newly-widowed Emma married him. She had apparently enjoyed her role as Lady of the English and was not about to surrender it. Also, she may have found Canute, who proved to be a strong, able ruler, more to her taste than her first husband, the "redeless" Ethelred. Emma's sons by Ethelred went to live with their relatives in Normandy and Emma bore her new husband a son, Hardicanute. But Canute already had a family. The mother of his first son stayed in Denmark, while Emma held sway in England. Two queens with sons, meant trouble when Canute died.

Rollo's descendants

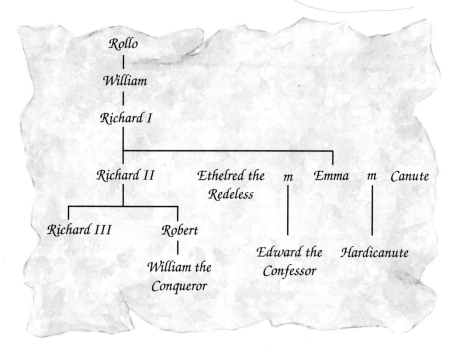

Norman conquests

In Normandy the descendants of Rollo, Viking chiefs now French dukes, settled down to control the activities of their troublemaking subjects. They were tough, active men, as ruthless as their Viking forebears, though now with a veneer of Christianity.

William became duke of Normandy in 1035 at the age of eight, when his father died. William had a very difficult and dangerous childhood, but somehow he survived the revolts and plots that threatened not only his inheritance but also his very life. In 1047 he had even managed to assert full control over his lands and his barons. He married his cousin, Matilda of Flanders, (who happened also to be a remote descendent of King Alfred the Great) but without the required permission of the pope. The two of them were excommunicated for a while, until they could get papal forgiveness for, and blessing on their union.

When Canute died, his sons failed to hold his empire together and in 1042 Edward, the surviving son of Ethelred the Redeless, returned to England as its king. But Edward, whose piety earned him the nickname "the Confessor," was half Norman and had spent so much time in Normandy that he felt more Norman than English. He offended his nobles by making little secret of his preference for Norman ways and the company of his Norman relatives and friends.

In 1051, William, duke of Normandy, visited Edward in England and there is little doubt that the childless king promised his throne to his young relative, though he had no power to do so. Nor is there any doubt that William was ambitious and wanted the crown, while his land-hungry barons wanted estates in England. The Viking spirit and piratical streak were running true to form.

When Edward died in 1066, the English decided to have a say in who should rule them. They certainly did not want the Norman duke William, and the heir by blood, Edward's great-nephew, was only a child. The English Witan (King's Council) decided that, with a national emergency brewing, England needed a grown man as ruler. They chose a powerful nobleman, Harold, earl of Wessex.

The decision came just in time. No sooner was Harold crowned than Harald Hardradi, king of Norway, claimed the English throne as the heir of Canute. He arrived off the northeast coast of England in September 1066 with a huge battle fleet.

The two kings met at Stamford Bridge and the Viking was defeated. But even as they were celebrating their victory over one Viking, the English got the news that the descendant of

Rollo's Vikings, having settled in Normandy, adopted the French method of fighting – on horseback – and this is how they defeated the English, who were mostly on foot.

The Last of the Vikings

Harald Hardradi (the Ruthless) was an extraordinary, larger-than-life character, whom some people have christened the Last Viking.

He was a member of the Norwegian royal family and in 1030, when he was still only 15, he was already fighting for his older brother Olaf. Olaf was killed, however, and Harald was forced to flee. He went to Kiev, in Russia, where he took service with the prince of Kiev, fighting in his many wars. Four years later he moved on to Constantinople and served in the Varangian Guard for nine years (see page 19).

Eventually he decided to go home. He passed through Kiev on the way back and married Elizabeth, the daughter of his former employer, the prince of Kiev.

Once back in Norway, he got his nephew King Magnus to accept him as co-ruler and when young Magnus died shortly afterward,

took the throne for himself. He spent the next 18 years in a series of bitter wars against the Danes, whose throne he felt (with little justification) should also be his. His claim to the throne of England was shaky in the extreme, but that did not stop him claiming that, too, on the death of Edward.

An 11th-century Byzantine painting of an emperor and his bodyguard outside a church. The Varangian Guard would have looked very similar.

Having conquered England, the Normans built castles like this one at Bamburgh in Northumberland to maintain their power over the Anglo-Saxons. The square keep is typical of early Norman castles.

another, Duke William, had invaded. Harold and his army, still tired from the last battle, force-marched south to their defeat at the historic Battle of Hastings. William the Norman became William the Conqueror, king of England. Many of the men who had come from Normandy with him were younger men, looking for lands of their own, just as their forefathers had done when they went to Normandy. They were not disappointed.

The migration south

It was not just the dukes of Normandy who were eager to extend their powers. The barons were also warlike and greedy, it seems. One particularly ambitious and energetic family were the de Hautevilles.

In 1017 Norman adventurers began arriving in southern Italy, with an eye to conquest in the good old Viking manner. Since the collapse of the Roman Empire this area and the neighboring island of Sicily had suffered badly. They had been invaded at various times by Ostrogoths, Lombards, Vandals, Byzantines, and Arabs. They provided a tempting target for a take-over by a determined, united group.

The struggle was a long one, but the deciding factor had been the arrival of Robert, son of Tancred de Hauteville. He had soon

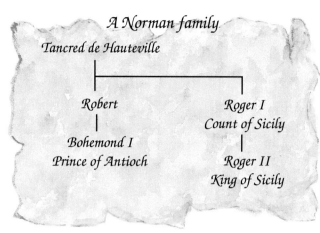

A Norman family

Tancred de Hauteville

Robert

Bohemond I
Prince of Antioch

Roger I
Count of Sicily

Roger II
King of Sicily

Krak des Chevaliers was built by the Christians in the Holy Land during the Crusades, the war against the Muslims. The descendants of Rollo's Vikings were among the most prominent leaders of the Crusades, including Robert's elder son.

emerged as the natural leader of the Normans and by 1050 they had succeeded in taking control of southern Italy. Pope Leo IX bitterly opposed this Norman take-over but, in typically ruthless fashion, Robert imprisoned Leo and "persuaded" the pope to recognize him as the duke of Apulia, a region of southeastern Italy.

In 1057 Roger, the youngest of Tancred's sons, arrived to help brother Robert in his newly-won duchy. However Robert had even more grandiose schemes. Five years later he made Roger count of Sicily, although it took Roger nearly 30 years to conquer the whole island.

While Roger was busy in Sicily, Robert's eyes were already on the eastern horizon. He had come into contact with the glories of the Byzantine Empire in southern Italy and it had whetted his appetite. Just as the Rus had looked longingly at the riches of Constantinople, so now did Robert. From 1080 till his death in 1085 he and his elder son, Bohemund, invaded the Byzantine provinces across the Adriatic. However these were eventually to prove too tough a nut, even for that grasping pair to crack.

In 1096 Bohemund joined the First Crusade as leader of a group of Normans from southern Italy. He played a decisive role in the capture of Antioch and would not give up that rich prize, establishing himself as its prince. His family held on stubbornly to Antioch until it was finally retaken by the Muslims in 1268, one of the last Crusader strongholds to fall.

At the death of Robert, Roger of Sicily became head of the House of Hauteville. When he died the role fell to his son, Roger II. Bohemund was by then fully occupied in the Holy Land and his younger brother inherited the title of duke of Apulia. By 1130 Roger II united the family lands in Sicily and the south of Italy, and the pope recognized him as king of Sicily. Yet another adventurer of Viking descent had carved himself out a kingdom. This inheritance was to survive as the Kingdom of the Two Sicilies right into the 19th century.

Roger II's luxurious and dazzling court at Palermo was a meeting place of Roman Catholic, Greek Orthodox, Muslim, and Jewish scholars. His daughter and heiress, Constance, married the Holy Roman emperor Henry VI, and their son was the emperor Frederick II. Frederick kept a firm grip on an empire that stretched from the Baltic through Germany and most of Italy. He was a man of great intelligence, whose unusual political and religious ideas won him both devoted supporters and bitter enemies and the nickname of Stupor Mundi – the Wonder of the World. A fitting epitaph for the heir to the genius and the fighting spirit of the Norsemen.

A coin showing Roger II.

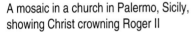

A mosaic in a church in Palermo, Sicily, showing Christ crowning Roger II

Horizons

Some of the other interesting people who lived about the same time as Eric and his family were: Elfrida, second wife of King Edgar of England; Hugh Capet, first king of the House of Capet; St. Dunstan, Archbishop of Canterbury; St. Adelaide, empress of the Holy Roman Empire; the Byzantine emperor Basil II, the "Bulgar Killer"; St. Vladimir, prince of Kiev; St. Stephen, first Christian king of Hungary.

And Afterward

A monk in his library. Even before the Viking Age, monks acted as record-keepers. Their writings help us to find out about the history of their time.

It is ironic that, while other Vikings ended up on thrones, Eric the Red and his family, who had explored the farthest horizons, and who had been the first Europeans to visit new lands in the West, should sink back into obscurity. Their discoveries and achievements were not rewarded with political power, and were largely forgotten by all save a few monks and the poets who preserved their deeds in the sagas.

The memory fades

The links with America were not, it seems, broken as soon as the family of Eric the Red ceased to travel there. However, evidence of contact is hard to come by, suggesting that visits were few and that they eventually ceased.

About 1075, the monk Adam of Bremen wrote a history of the archbishops of Hamburg. In it he mentions Vinland (claiming his information came from no less a person than the king of Denmark), praising the grapes and self-sown wheat found there. Vinland was therefore still very much "on the map" in Adam's day.

An entry in the Icelandic Annals for 1121 says a bishop Eric set out from Greenland for Vinland. But as Greenland did not have a bishop till a few years later and no Bishop Eric is known, this information is a bit doubtful.

Later in the same century an Icelandic monk produced a work on geography that mentions all three of Leif's ports of call – Helluland, Markland, and Vinland – but he clearly knew little about them apart from their names. In 1225, a Norwegian scholar completed his history of the kings of Norway, which contains quite a bit of information about Vinland. Most of it, however, seems to have been drawn from the sagas that were being written down at this time, so it cannot be taken as independent or contemporary evidence.

There is, however, one good, very interesting reference, to contact with America, dated 1347. It tells how a Greenland ship was on the way home from Markland when it was blown off course and arrived in Iceland instead. Since Markland was "Forest-land," it may well be that, desperate for timber, some Greenlanders still made voyages to Leif's new lands.

We have already seen that the Norsemen still went on exploring the northern lands, reaching up into the Arctic Circle.

In 1194 one Icelandic ship, we are told, discovered land five days' sail to the north. They called it Svalbard – Cold Coast – which may well have been the island of Spitzbergen, while in 1285 two brothers from Iceland explored land to the west, which was probably the little-visited east coast of Greenland.

The failure of the Greenland colonies made any explorations in that area much less likely, but the existence of Greenland itself was well-known in Europe, though very few had visited it, even when the colonies there were flourishing. As late as 1492, Pope Alexander VI was wondering whether the bishop-elect of Gardar ought actually to visit Greenland!

Eyes West

When might knowledge about the discovery of Vinland have become known outside Scandinavia? Is it possible that Christopher Columbus might have heard some whisper about it? It has to be acknowledged that, though just possible, it is, on the present evidence, unlikely. Though many people knew about Greenland in 15th-century Europe, it is very doubtful if Vinland was remembered, unless it was by the Icelanders. Even in Iceland, by the 15th century, it might well have been thought of as mythical – the sagas had long since been forgotten. The most that can be said is that, by that time, the knowledge that there were islands in the Atlantic – the Canaries, Madeira, and the Azores in the south, Iceland and Greenland in the north – sharpened the interest of the new generation of explorers emerging in Portugal, Castile (now part of Spain), and later England.

By the 15th century, the ships used for exploration – and for war – had changed from the Viking designs. This painting shows the raised forecastle at the bow of the ship, used as a fighting platform.

And yet, the doubt still remains: amid all of the reports and rumors of strange lands out across the Atlantic that Columbus heard, had he also heard about Vinland? Would it have helped strengthen his belief that the Indies could be reached by sailing west? That it was not too far away? Trade did continue with Iceland, so rumors, however garbled, may have got back.

Then there is the tantalizing case of two ships from Bristol that found, somewhere to the west of Ireland "a certain island called Brasil." In 1481 there was an official inquiry into this voyage in Bristol. Then, in 1497, a London merchant, Hugh Say, wrote, apparently to Christopher Columbus himself, shortly after his second voyage, referring to the discovery of "Brasil" – "as your lordship well knows." Does that refer to the 1481 discovery and if so, did Columbus "well know" of it before he sailed in 1492? Unprovable at the moment, but a fascinating thought.

Greenland revisited

Before the Viking communities in Greenland collapsed, they had accepted the rule first of the Norwegian crown (in 1261), then of the Danish crown (in 1380). In 1712, some 300 years after Greenland had been abandoned, the king of Denmark and Norway sent an expedition under a clergyman to bring encouragement to the supposedly Christian descendants of the Vikings, believed to be living there. They did not find any, of course, only Eskimos. However, a link between Denmark and Greenland was established and a new period of contact began. In 1979 Greenland became a self-governing community under the Danish crown.

Did St. Brendan beat the Vikings?

The Irish Saga, the Voyage of St. Brendan the Abbot, tells how St. Brendan and 17 monks set sail (sometime before A.D.600). They headed westward across the Atlantic in a skin-covered boat (the same Irish curragh which is still made today by some Irish fishermen). According to the story, they visited a number of

Volcanoes (top), icebergs (right), and whales (below) must have startled early explorers who saw them for the first time.

islands, each more extraordinary than the last. They also encountered great marvels such as demons who hurled fire at them, a crystal column that floated on the sea, a thick white cloud through which they had to sail, and a sea monster as big as an island that nearly upset the boat. They eventually reached a continent that some later claimed must have been America. After a short stay they returned home to Ireland. The round trip had taken seven years.

Most people dismissed the whole story as a fable – floating crystals columns, fire-hurling demons, and all. But a few people felt there might be more to it. Of course, over many years of being passed on by word of mouth, the story would have been exaggerated and even true aspects would have been distorted and misunderstood, but the central fact might be true. After all, the later Irish monks and the Vikings did island-hop across the North Atlantic and the strange "miracles" encountered by Brendan and his crew could be quite ordinary things that had been misinterpreted or misunderstood. The fire-hurling demons could be a volcano on Iceland, the crystal column could be an iceberg, the thick white cloud fog and the monstrous sea

The Brendan being built and (right) at sea.

creature a whale. But could a leather-covered curragh actually make it across the Atlantic? Timothy Severin and a four-man crew decided to prove it could. They set sail in May 1976 in a specially built 40-foot long, open boat made of leather on a wooden frame, which they called *The Brendan* in honor of the saint. And they made it. It took more than a year and much danger, hardship, and boredom, but they did it. So St. Brendan and his companions *could* have made the journey. But that is quite different from being able to prove that they did, and we have no proof. It must remain an intriguing mystery – unless someone, somewhere, finds some more concrete evidence.

Fables, fantasies, and fakes

Over the centuries since Eric and Leif, there have been many other stories of claims by Europeans to have discovered America. There is the story of a Welsh prince called Madoc, said to have colonized America in the 12th century. This seems to have been a story invented in the 16th century. It was probably intended to give the Tudors, the ruling family of England, and of Welsh ancestry, a claim to the lands in the New World. This would have put them a step ahead of Columbus.

Another highly suspect claim is that, in the 14th century, an English monk called Nicholas of Lynn visited both Greenland and Vinland and wrote about them. The first reference to his epic voyage does not occur until the late 15th century (once again after Columbus's voyage in 1492). Anyway, the real Nicholas of Lynn does not seem to have traveled anywhere, let alone across the Atlantic. His voyages, like those of Madoc, are fantasies.

In 1892 there were great celebrations to mark the 400th anniversary of Columbus's first voyage. The Americans of Scandinavian origin, determined not to be outdone, revived the stories of Eric and Leif, and, a replica of the Gokstad ship was sailed across the Atlantic a year later. There were many Scandinavian settlers in Minnesota and, to no one's surprise, there in 1898, at a place called Kensington, a stone inscribed with runes was found. It apparently recorded the presence there in 1362 of a party of Swedes and Norwegians. The stone (despite passionate support by some) has been shown to be a forgery, made only a little while before it was "discovered."

The Vinland Map

In 1965 in the United States, Yale University proudly announced the acquisition of an antique map, dated 1440. It showed the world (or as much of it as was then known) drawn in the style of other maps of the period, but with two startling differences – it showed Greenland in excellent detail and the "Island of Vinland." Naturally, everyone was very excited. Someone else had reached America more than 50 years before Columbus and had known the name Vinland and had drawn a map!

Some experts, however, were worried by the map. Where did it come from? It had just appeared a few years before from nowhere, with no history to back it up. How could people have possibly drawn the outline of Greenland so perfectly? Had they sailed right around it? An impossible feat, surely, so far north, so early. Why were there mistakes in the Latin? Heated arguments took place. Was the map genuine or a forgery? It was decided to

The Vinland Map.

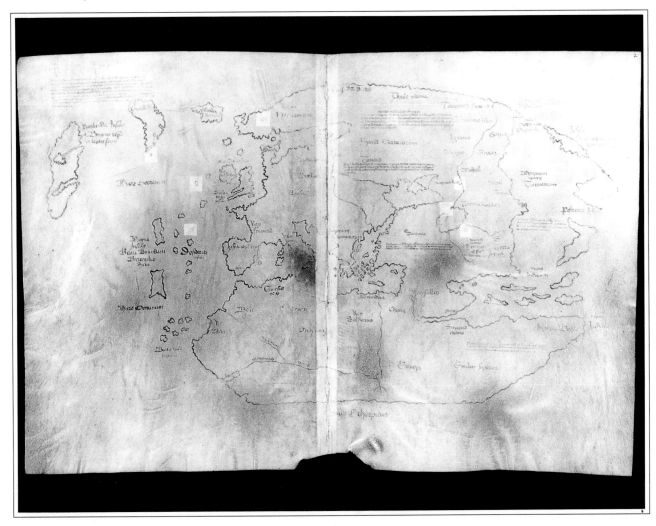

settle matters one way or another. In 1972 tests were run on the map. The ink was found to contain a coloring substance called titanium dioxide in a form that was not available until the 20th century. The Vinland Map was a fake.

Archaeologists have found remains of Brattahlid, at the Eastern Settlement, which was founded by Eric the Red.

But the Vinland Map had enthusiastic supporters. In 1984 more sophisticated, modern tests were done on the ink. The titanium dioxide was shown to be present but only in minute quantities (5,000 times less than the original tests had suggested). So that was not what had been used to color it. Unhappily, that still does not make the map genuine. Much more positive evidence would be needed to do that and most scholars still believe it to be a very clever forgery.

Archaeology to the rescue

A few genuine, isolated Viking objects have been found in America over the years but (apart from odd items left by the early Viking explorers of the Arctic) they all seem to have been brought over from Scandinavia in the 19th century. They were planted as jokes or as attempts to prove Viking presence. Or they were simply misplaced and found later by people who really believed the objects had been in place for hundreds of years.

Looking for a short-lived Viking colony somewhere on the east coast of America, when we are not even sure which areas Leif and his successors visited, is indeed like searching through a haystack for the proverbial needle. But in 1960 such a site was discovered at L'Anse aux Meadows (see page 29). Excavations there have revealed a genuine Viking settlement. The houses closely resemble those in Greenland, a few hand-made Norse objects have been found, and scientific carbon-14 tests show that they could date back to the 11th century. L'Anse aux Meadows was, therefore, briefly occupied by Vikings, but whether they were Leif and his family or some other, forgotten heroes, we have no way of knowing at present. Who knows what archaeologists may find tomorrow, or next year, or some time after that?

Glossary

Byzantines Inhabitants of the Byzantine Empire, which was originally the eastern half of the Roman Empire. Its capital was called Byzantium, then Constantinople and is now called Istanbul.

carbon-14 test A scientific method of dating organic remains (*e.g.* plants, trees, bones) by measuring the decay of radioactive carbon, known as carbon 14, which is found in all living material but which decays after death.

Celtic women Celtic peoples were once found living throughout most of Western Europe. They spoke closely-related Celtic languages. At the time of the Vikings, their descendants lived in Ireland, Wales, Scotland, Cornwall, and Brittany. The Celtic women who were taken to Iceland were from Ireland and perhaps Scotland.

chronicle A written record of events in the order they happened.

circumnavigation A journey completely around something, usually to sail around an island or the world.

colonist A person who sets up home in a new country.

colony A settlement established by a group of people in a new country.

Crusade A holy war. One of several fought by European Christians to recover the Holy Land from the Muslims.

Franks People from across the eastern frontier of the Roman Empire who conquered what is now France in the 6th century A.D.

Islam The faith proclaimed by the Prophet Mohammed.

merchant A trader, especially one who trades with foreign countries.

migration A journey by people from their own homeland in order to settle in a new land.

pagan A person who is not a member of one of the world's most widely-supported religions. In this context, especially one who is not either a Christian, Jew, or Muslim.

patriarch A very high-ranking priest in the Orthodox Church.

Renaissance A revival of interest in the art, architecture, and learning of Greece and Rome that began in 15th-century Italy and spread through Europe.

Roman Empire The city of Rome, founded in the 8th century B.C., had united Italy under its rule by the end of the 3rd century B.C. From then on it embarked on the conquest of a vast empire. At its greatest extent, in the 2nd century A.D., it covered most of Europe, North Africa, and the Middle East. It was divided into two parts, West and East, by the emperor Diocletian (284–305). In 476 the emperor Romulus Augustus was deposed. This marks the end of the Western part of the Empire. The Eastern part, later known as the Byzantine Empire, continued until 1453 when its capital, Constantinople, was captured by Muslim Turks.

Further Reading

Atkinson, I. *The Viking Ships*. Cambridge University Press, 1979

Birkett, Alaric. *Vikings*. Dufour Editions, 1985

Colum, Padraic. *The Children of Odin: The Book of Northern Myths*. Macmillan, 1984

Daly, Kathleen N. *Norse Mythology A to Z*. Facts on File, 1990

The Early Middle Ages, "History of the World" series. Raintree Steck-Vaughn, 1992

Frost, Abigail. *The Age of Chivalry*. Marshall Cavendish Corp., 1990

Humble, Richard. *The Age of Leif Eriksson*. Watts, 1989

Leon, George D. *Explorers of the Americas Before Columbus*. Watts, 1990

Martell, Hazel M. *The Vikings*. Macmillan, 1992

—— *The Vikings & Jorvik*. Macmillan, 1993

Mulvihill, Margaret. *Viking Longboats*. Watts, 1989

Odijk, Pamela. *The Vikings*. Silver Burdett Press, 1990

Schiller, Barbara. *Eric the Red & Leif the Lucky*. Troll Assocs., 1979

Simon, Charman. *Leif Eriksson & the Vikings: The Norse Discovery of America*. Childrens Press, 1991

Speed, Peter. *Life in the Time of Harald Hardrada and the Vikings*, "Life in the Time of" series. Raintree Steck-Vaughn, 1993

Stainer, Tom and Sutton, Harry. *The Vikings*. Parkwest Pubns., 1992

Stefoff, Rebecca. *The Viking Explorers*. Chelsea House, 1993

Viking Sailor. Rourke Corp., 1987

Vikings. Harcourt Brace, 1992

Index

Note: Page numbers in italics indicate illustrations.

keel, ship's, 12
Kensington, stone at, 41-42
kerling, 13
Kiev, 34
Kingdom of the Two Sicilies, 37
kingdoms, Scandinavian, 7
Krak des Chevaliers, *36*

land
    shortage of, 4, 11
    travel on, *8*
L'Anse aux Meadows, 28, *29*, 43
L'Anse aux Méduse (Jellyfish Creek), 28
Leif the Lucky, 25, 26-27, 38, 41
Leo IX, Pope, 36
Lombards, 35
longships, 13-14, *15*

Madeira Islands, 39
Madoc, 41
Magnus, King (Norway), 34
Magyars, 6
Markland (Forest-land), 26, 38
    Labrador as, 27, *28*
mast fish, 13
Matilda of Flanders, 33
Mecca, *6*
Mediterranean Sea, *18*
memorial stones, Viking, *12, 23*
mercenaries, 19
merchant(s), 7, 39
    ships of, 14
    traveling, 9
merchant ships, Viking, 14
migration, 4
    southward, 35-36
Miklagard, 19
Minnesota, Scandinavian settlers in, 41-42
Mohammed, 6
monks
    as explorers, 20, 21
    as record keepers, *38*
mosaic, *19*
Muslims, 6, 36, 37

Native Americans, and Vikings, 29
navigational skills, Viking, 16
Newfoundland, as Vinland, 28
Nicholas of Lynn, 41
Njord, 9
Normandy, 18
    Vikings in, 33-34
Norsemen, 4
    as sailors/boat men, 12
    See also Vikings
North Sea, *18*
Norway and Norwegians
    colonize Iceland, 21
    conversion of, 11
    history of kings of, 38
    on Scottish islands, 20
    settlements of, 19
    terrain of, 7

oats, 8
Odin, 5, 7, 9, *10*
Orkney Islands, 20
Oseberg ship, *12,* 14
Ostrogoths, 35
outlawry, sentence of, 22

pirates, Viking, 4
polar bears, 24
population, growth in, 4, 7, 11
Pytheas of Marseilles, 20-21

Ragnarok, 10
raids and raiders, Vikings, 4, 7, 16-17
Redeless, as term, 32
Richard I, Duke of Normandy, 33
Roger II, King (Sicily), *37*
Rollo, 18
    descendants of, *33*
Roman Empire, collapse of, 6
runes, 5, 24, 41-42
Rurik, 19
Russia, 19
rye, 8

sacrifices, Viking, 10
sagas, 5, 38
salt, need for, 9
Say, Hugh, 39
Scandinavia and the Vikings, 6-7
    as boat builders, 12
    conversion of, 24
Scotland, Vikings raid, 20
seabirds, 8
seals, 8
Sea of Marmara, *18,* 19
self-government, 24-25, 40
Severin, Timothy, 41
Shetland Islands, 20
Shi'ite party, 6
ships, 12-15, *39*
Sicily, 35
    de Hautevilles conquer, 36, 37
silk cloth, 9
skates, *8*
Skraelings, 29, 30, 31
Slavs, territories of, 19
sledges, 8
Snorri, 30
Spitzbergen, 39
Stamford Bridge, 34
starboard, as term, 14
Stephen, King (Hungary), *6*
strakes, of boat, 12-13, *15*
Stupor Mundi (Wonder of the World), 37
styra, as term, 14
Sunni party, 6
Svalbard, 39
Sweden and the Swedish, 7
    conversion of, 11
    settlements of, 19
    terrain of, 7
Sweyn Forkbeard, King (Denmark), 32

The Brendan, 41
Thing, defined, 22
Thjodhild (wife of Eric), 22, 25
Thor, 7, 9, *10*
Thorfinn, 29
    in Vinland, 30
Thorir, 27, 29
Thorstein (son of Eric), 25, 29
Thorvald (son of Eric), 25, 28-29
Thorvaldsson, Eric, 4
    See also Eric the Red
Thorvard (son-in-law of Eric), 30, 31
Thule, 20-21
    See also Iceland
timber, as import, 24, 25
trade and traders
    with Iceland, 39
    at Jorvik, *32*
    Viking, 4, 7
    in Vinland, 30
travel, Viking, 8

Valhalla, 10
Valkyries, 10
Vandals, 35
Varangian Guard, 19, 34
Vikings
    as boat builders, 12-15
    carvings of, *12, 15*
    classes of society of, 7
    expand westward, 20
    houses of, 8
    nine worlds of, 10
    origin of, 6-7
    origin of term, 11
    as raiders, 4, 11, 16-17
    self-sufficiency of, 8-9
    take-over, 17-19
    as warriors, 4, 6, 11
    worship practices of, 9-10
Vinland, 26-32
    mention of, 38
    question of location of, 27-28
Vinland Map, *42*
Vladimir, St., prince of Kiev, 19
Voyage of St. Brendan the Abbot, 40

walruses, 8, *24*
weapons, Viking, *4,* 9
wergild, 22
Western Settlement, 24, 25, *26,* 29
whales, 8, 24
wheat, 8
William, Duke of Normandy (William the Conqueror),18, 33-35
    conquers England, 35
Witan (Council), 13, 34

Yggdrasill, 10
York, England, *5, 32*